MAKE MONEY!

WASH
CARS

Bridget Heos **Illustrated by Daniele Fabbri**

Amicus Illustrated is published by Amicus
P.O. Box 1329, Mankato, MN 56002
www.amicuspublishing.us

Library of Congress Cataloging-in-Publication Data
Heos, Bridget.
 Make money! Wash cars / by Bridget Heos;
illustrated by Daniele Fabbri.
    pages cm. — (Make money!)
 Summary: "Through trial and error and a few
humorous mistakes, a boy learns how to wash cars, find
customers, and create a successful car wash business
to earn enough money to buy a new skateboard"—
Provided by publisher.
 ISBN 978-1-60753-364-1 (library binding) —
ISBN 978-1-60753-412-9 (ebook)
1. Automobiles–Cleaning–Juvenile literature. 2. Car
washes–Juvenile literature. 3. Money-making projects
for children–Juvenile literature. I. Fabbri, Daniele,
illustrator. II. Title.
 TL152.15.H46 2014
 629.2'60288–dc23
                                    2012050631

Editor: Rebecca Glaser
Designer: The Design Lab

Printed in the United States of America at
Corporate Graphics in North Mankato, Minnesota.

Date 2/2013   PO 1147

10 9 8 7 6 5 4 3 2 1

That's a cool set of wheels. But a new skateboard costs $80. How could you earn that much?

A car wash!

You'll need soap. Not dish soap. It can damage the car's paint. Car wash soap works. But it can damage the local stream.

Use eco-friendly car wash soap. Good business owners care about their neighbors—even the fish and frogs!

You'll also need a sponge for scrubbing and a soft towel for drying. Maybe your mom would take you to the hardware store.

"Mom, can I borrow $10 to buy car washing supplies?"

"Yes. You can pay me back by washing my car."

Exchanging goods and services is called bartering. It's a very old way of doing business.

Time to get started. You owe your mom a good car wash. And when people see her gleaming car, they'll know you do good work. Wash and rinse from top to bottom.

Even if it's a warm day, don't let the car air-dry. It will get streaks. Use a soft towel instead.

Now that you've gotten some practice, you can wash your neighbors' cars.

You could put out a sign. But they might not see it.

You could make business cards. Pass them out door-to-door. Be polite. Explain your services. Tell them you charge $10 per car. Wow! Three customers. You'll be busy all afternoon.

Your third customer is Mrs. Tanke. She wants the inside of her car cleaned. She'll pay you an extra $10.

But peek inside first.

Ask her to take out anything she wants to keep. Now throw away trash and vacuum and wipe down the car.

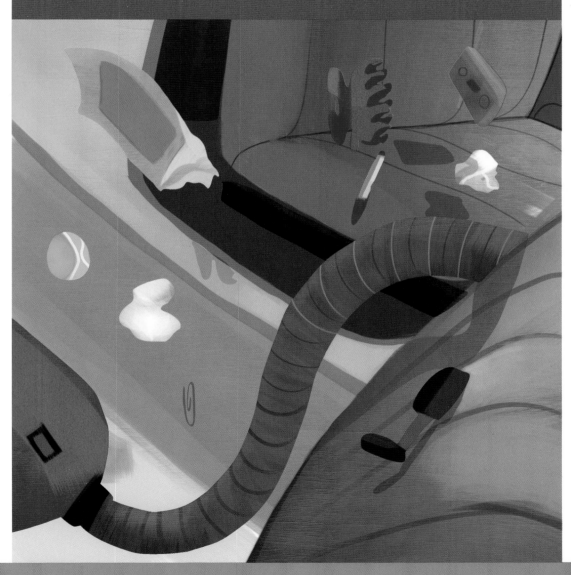

Mr. Mueller lives next door. He wants his car detailed. That involves special cleaners and tools.

It's okay to turn down a job you don't know how to do. Later, you might decide to learn these skills.

You're tired, but you've made $40 in one day! It's not enough for the skateboard. You've knocked on every door on your block. Better luck next time.

Wait. Your friend Jaden likes making money. Tomorrow, you could ask if he wants to wash cars with you on his block and split the cash.

Jaden agrees to be your business partner. You find four customers on his block and make $40 in half the time. But remember, you need to split that. You each get $20.

$$40/2 =$$
20 me   20 Jaden

Why not try again next Saturday?
You and Jaden find four more customers.

Now, you've each made $40. You have $80 total, enough for the skateboard. Jaden has enough for a new helmet and some skateboard stickers.

Time to take your own set of wheels for a spin!

Counting Your Money!

If you start a car wash business, keep track of how much you make. Here's a sample based on this story.

```
FIRST SATURDAY
Wash 3 cars                $30.00
Wash 1 car interior        $10.00

SUNDAY
Wash 4 cars                $40.00
Give half to partner      - 20.00

SECOND SATURDAY
Wash 4 cars                $40.00
Give half to partner      - 20.00

TOTAL
You                        $80.00
Your partner               $40.00
```

Glossary

bartering Exchanging goods or services.

business partner One who shares the responsibility and profits of a business.

customer A person who buys or might buy what you're selling.

eco-friendly Not harmful to the environment.

service A task that someone is paid to do for others.

supplies Items you need to do a job.

Read More

Antill, Sara. *10 Ways I Can Earn Money*. New York: PowerKids Press, 2012.

Bair, Sheila. Ill. by Judy Stead. *Isabel's Car Wa$h*. New York: AV2 by Weigl, 2012.

Orr, Tamra. *A Kid's Guide to Earning Money*. Hockessin, Del.: Mitchell Lane, 2009.

Web Sites

It's My Life: Money
http://pbskids.org/itsmylife/money/
Learn how to earn, save, and spend wisely.

Money for Kids: Making Money
http://www.kidsmoney.org/makemone.htm
Read advice from other kids who have tried earning money.

National Geographic Kids: Car Wash Kit
http://kids.nationalgeographic.com/kids/ activities/crafts/kit-car-wash/
Collect all the supplies you need and make a car wash kit.

About the Author

Bridget Heos is the author of more than 30 books for children, but made her millions babysitting in grade school and high school. She once babysat for a parrot who loved watching T.V. He would say, "Turn on Nick at Nite!"

About the Illustrator

Daniele Fabbri was born in Ravenna, Italy, in 1978. He graduated from Istituto Europeo di Design in Milan, Italy, and started his career as cartoon animator, storyboarder, and background designer for animated series. He has worked as a freelance illustrator since 2003, collaborating with international publishers and advertising agencies.